One of the most attractive examples of steam rollers produced by the large German manufacturers Maffei of Munich and Leipzig is this 1927 single-cylinder example, number 9193. It stands adjacent to the Technical Buildings in Freiburg, near Dresden, Germany, and, although not steamable, is kept in good order. It is one of the few survivors of this marque which has a steam dome in front of the cylinder block — an unusual feature to British eyes.

ROAD ROLLERS

Derek Rayner

Shire Publications Ltd

CONTENTS

Printed in Great Britain by C. I. Thomas & Sons (Haverfordwest) Ltd, Press Buildings, Merlins Bridge, Haverfordwest, Dyfed SA61 1XF.

British Library Cataloguing in Publication Data: Rayner, Derek A. Road Rollers — (Shire Albums; No. 281). I. Title. II. Series. 629.22. ISBN 0-7478-0153-3.

ACKNOWLEDGEMENTS

The author wishes to record his thanks to Lyndon R. Shearman, President of the Road Roller Association and one of the last roller owner-drivers in Britain, for his help, advice and encouragement during the preparation of this book; and to the Road Roller Association for permission to use illustrations from its extensive archive collection. Illustrations are acknowledged as follows: Aveling-Barford Archives, pages 2, 4 and 7; B. G. Bartram, page 24; R. Griffin, page 3; Hampshire Brothers, pages 5, 21 (bottom), 22 (top) and 23 (top); Institute of Agricultural History and Museum of English Rural Life, University of Reading, pages 6, 12 and 22 (bottom); R. G. Pratt, pages 2, 15 (bottom), 20 (top) and 21 (top); Road Roller Association, pages 9 (bottom), 10-11 (all), 13 (both), 16-19 (all), 23 (bottom), 26 (top left), 27-32 (all); B. Roberts, page 9 (top); R. Verhoeven, pages 1 and 14; P. N. Williams, pages 15 (top) and 20 (bottom). The remaining photographs are from the author's collection.

Cover: Aveling & Porter steam roller number 2481 was built in Rochester, Kent, in 1889 and photographed at the Harewood House Steam Rally near Leeds in 1990. It is a single-cylinder machine and weighs 10 tons in working order. During its working life it was employed by Cambridge Corporation and features an early type of steering mechanism where the chains are fixed to small drums, known as bobbins, on either side of the boiler. The rear roll scrapers are balanced by weights.

Below: Aveling's first steam roller was a converted traction engine which had its normal road wheels replaced by extra-wide smooth wheels, 7 feet (2134 mm) in diameter and 3 feet (915 mm) wide. The experimental machine was tried out in Hyde Park, London, in 1865. Its weight was around 20 tons.

This steam roller was photographed in October 1983 in Datong, China, not far from the main railway workshops, which at that time were still producing steam locomotives. It is believed to be a mid 1950s local product although it bore little evidence of its date of building or manufacturer.

INTRODUCTION

The steam roller, although conceived in France, is a piece of engineering as typically British as the game of cricket. The developed idea of such a vehicle was subsequently copied worldwide and it is undoubtedly the best known and easiest recalled product of the steam age on the road, since it lasted longest. Rollers powered by steam were still being built in Germany, France and China until the early 1950s. Motor rollers are still often referred to as steam rollers, so well established is the image conjured up by the term. Indeed the machine has become much used by the comic scriptwriter to raise a laugh. 'Steamroller' has even been taken into the language as a verb meaning to squash the opposition.

It was the humble steam roller that gave most of the roads of today their first compacted foundations and good running surface. Steam rollers were in use from 1865 up to the mid 1960s and lasted just long enough to be used in parts during the construction of the first motorway in Britain, the M1.

When they first appeared, motor rollers were in competition with steam rollers. Indeed, the two types were manufactured concurrently for road construction for the first fifty years of the twentieth century and continued in use side by side for a further fifteen. Steam rollers were finally ousted in the mid 1960s, invariably when the old drivers retired. Younger men were unhappy with the total lack of creature comforts on steam rollers and did not have the skills needed to operate and maintain them. More steam rollers have survived into the preservation era than any other type of road steam vehicle, mainly because of their durability and the fact that they were capable of doing as good a job as a motor-powered machine. Many enthusiasts now enjoy owning a steam roller. As prices of these rise, vintage motor rollers are being bought as acceptable alternatives in a similar way to the progression from traction engines to vintage tractors in another field of preservation.

The term 'vintage' is applied in some enthusiast circles to vehicles 25 years old or more, but when applied to road rollers it is generally accepted to include those rollers built before or during the Second World War and also those built after but to essentially pre-war designs. It is these which form the basis of this book. Modern rollers date from around 1950 and are not considered in detail.

3

One of Thomas Aveling's first steam rollers was this 30 ton example which had a 500 gallon (2273 litre) water tank over the hind roll and was steered by a ship's handwheel. Despite its bulk it is said that it could be turned in its own length. This illustration from the 'Illustrated London News' of 12th October 1867 shows the roller working in Liverpool.

PIONEERING DEVELOPMENTS

To assist in the movement of people and goods around Britain as a result of the industrial revolution, the existing roads required a better surface for the wheeled vehicles of the time, which were increasing in weight as they were expected to carry greater loads for longer distances. Telford and Macadam relied on road traffic to compact the new roadway. When rollers came into use the only means of propulsion was man power or a team of horses. Transport by rail had been revolutionised by the invention of the railway locomotive and it was logical therefore that steam power should be used for traction on the roads and then as a means of propulsion for road rollers.

The steam roller originated in France, where, independently it would appear, Lemoine of Bordeaux and Ballaison of Paris built machines which were trialled in the Bois de Boulogne near Paris in 1860 and 1861 respectively. Although these machines did not look alike, both had horizontal boilers. These rollers were success-

ful but were large machines. The first steam roller to be built in Britain was the joint design of W. Clark, Chief Engineer of the Municipality of Calcutta, and W. F. Batho of Birmingham. This was a huge machine weighing some 30 tons and was shipped in 1863 to India, where it worked successfully for a time.

Meanwhile Thomas Aveling, a Kentish farmer with an eye for engineering, had seen the horse-drawn portable engine come into general use for driving farm machinery in the early 1850s and in 1859 he devised a means of making it self-moving. The first of these new engines was a Clayton and Shuttleworth portable, modified by that firm for him. In 1862 he founded, with Richard T. Porter, the firm of Aveling & Porter at Rochester, Kent, and he later decided that steam power could be applied to roadmaking. In 1865 he designed and built the first steam roller to be used in Britain. This was the forerunner of some twenty thousand rollers produced by

Hampshire Brothers' McLaren convertible steam roller number 287 'Harvester' of 1886 in the heavy woollen district of West Yorkshire about 1910. Tom Hampshire is the young man by the rear roll. This roller was so sturdily built that when it was cut up in July 1939 the boiler plates were as good as new.

the firm and its successors, all bearing the emblem of the rampant horse of Kent above the *Invicta* scroll. As the century progressed, the steam roller became an essential and much used tool of the roadmaker.

The first vehicles driven by internal combustion engines spluttered on to the roads towards the 1890s and a similar transition occurred. When such engines had developed sufficiently to be applied to other purposes, they were installed in road rollers in the hope of making them more efficient. Motor rollers have therefore been in existence since the early years of the twentieth century. From the outset, there was competition between makers of steam and motor rollers so that developments took place in many respects almost simultaneously. Eventually the race was won by the motor roller, mainly because of its ease of use and economy.

The Aveling & Porter steam roller was developed into the conventional-looking machine which we know in preservation today within the first ten years of its existence, following an early penchant for very

heavy rollers of around 20 and 30 tons. Thomas Aveling patented the hornplates, the extension upwards of the flat sides of the firebox on which could be mounted the bearings for the crankshaft and other drive shafts without putting an unnecessary strain on the boiler. The front of the machine initially had small rollers pivoted beneath the smokebox and this arrangement was soon followed by a pair of larger rolls, firstly with an inverted T-shaped support with conical rolls and then an upturned U bracket through an extension of the smokebox with two parallel rolls. This eventually became the heavy cast front bracket — the forecarriage head — bolted on to the front of the smokebox.

Single-cylindered rollers consumed a lot of coal and water and it was Aveling, virtually simultaneously with the Leeds manufacturer John Fowler & Company Limited of the Steam Plough Works, Hunslet, who first introduced the compounding system. This uses the steam twice, firstly in a small cylinder at a high pressure and then in a larger cylinder at a lower pressure, before it

One of the first motor rollers — the French design of Coutant-Dujour fitted with the English 'Dudbridge' oil engine made in Stroud, Gloucestershire. Its total weight was around 17 tons. (Photograph taken from the 'Implement and Machinery Review', 2nd May 1902.)

is finally expelled up the chimney to pull the draught through the fire to make it burn well. This development was introduced on both traction engines and rollers in 1881, although Aveling's arrangement of tandem compound, with the cylinders set one in front of the other, was dropped almost immediately afterwards.

In Fowler's design the cylinders were side by side with cranks set at right angles on the crankshaft. This necessitated a wide area of the crankshaft being taken up with valve eccentrics and also the two big end crank brasses. A new design of compounding was introduced in 1889 by Charles Burrell & Sons, to the patented design of their chief draughtsman, Frederick J. Burrell. This became known as the single-crank compound and involved the same compounding arrangement of using the steam twice but the high-pressure cylinder was set diagonally above the lower one, making the casting rather taller but effectively reducing the centre line dimension of the cylinder. This also allowed both pistons to be coupled to a single crosshead, which meant that one connecting rod only, along with one set of eccentrics, was able to drive the arrangement. The main advantage of this new design was its economy and relative simplicity compared with the more conventional compound-cylindered engines. Although this was more essential

for traction engines used extensively to drive machinery by belt for long periods and also on long-distance road work, it was nevertheless just as relevant for rollers and a considerable number of such machines were sold. This arrangement was copied on the continent, possibly infringing patent rights, notably by the German firm of Ruthemeyer.

Other traction-engine manufacturers who started making steam rollers later in the nineteenth century were Thomas Green & Son of Leeds and Wallis & Steevens of Basingstoke, Hampshire. To make the purchase of a piece of equipment such as this viable it was necessary to get the best use out of it. Some contractors required an engine for one part of the year and a roller for the other. Hence the idea of a convertible engine was conceived, one on which the wheels could be changed to enable it to perform rolling jobs with its smooth wheels in summer and haulage and threshing jobs, with straked wheels, in the autumn and winter. A complete new front end could be bolted on to the front of a traction engine, in the form of a detachable forecarriage head, to enable the rolls and front forks to be fitted. The changeover from traction engine to roller could be effected in around a day with some jacks and lifting gear and created a versatile engine which found favour in many quarters.

Road rollers driven by internal combustion engines date from the late 1890s when a French contractor, Coutant-Dujour, built two oil-engined rollers. Unfortunately the French-built engines proved unsuccessful and he consequently ordered two oil engines from a British firm, Humpidge, Holborrow & Company of Dudbridge Ironworks, Stroud, Gloucestershire, to replace them. They supplied their standard 16 horsepower engines for this purpose. These were fitted with a specially designed bedplate and also equipped with their special vaporising device. This was the first successful application of a British oil engine to a motor roller.

It was reported in *The Engineer* of March 1902 that the two rollers fitted with Dudbridge engines had worked well near Paris for at least two years. They were built at Champeaux to a design patented by Coutant-Dujour and his partner Emile Salmson. The total weight of the roller in working order was around 17 tons.

The idea of having a slow-running single-cylinder oil engine driving a heavy three-wheel roller was first taken up in the British Isles in 1905 when J. G. Allen & Company of the Irish Road Engineering Works, Comber, County Down (and also of Islandbridge, Dublin), produced a roller very similar to the French-built machines. Whether this was an independent simultaneous development or an improvement of the previous ones has not been established but it does appear to have been the earliest example in the United Kingdom of an internal combustion-engined roller offered for commercial sale.

It was claimed that the 15 ton machine could run for a day on 8 gallons (30 litres) of oil, which at that time was priced at 5d per gallon, giving a cost of 3s 4d for an eight-hour day. A ton of oil, stored in the roller's tanks and the attendant living van, would last for over a month. Other advantages claimed were that only a few gallons of water were required each day and, more

A very early Barford & Perkins motor roller, number B018, as built in 1910. The absence of water tanks indicates that it was built for sports-ground work. The front rolls of this semi-tandem type are of the water-ballast variety.

importantly, that it took only fifteen minutes to start work from cold in a morning — a big saving in time over a steam roller. Because the single-cylinder oil engine had, of necessity, a large flywheel and was governed appropriately, the roller was capable of emulating a steam engine and could be used to drive other equipment such as a stone crusher. It could also be fitted with a scarifier for pulling up the road or used to haul an independent scarifier for the same purpose.

Small rollers were required for such duties as rolling sports fields, the drives of large houses and wide footpaths. After the passing of the Locomotive Act of 1896, which led to the introduction of small steam tractors, several traction-engine manufacturers made steam-roller versions of these. However, because of their size, they were difficult to handle and were used almost solely by councils rather than contractors.

Two firms, Barford & Perkins of Peterborough and Thomas Green of Leeds, were both at this time doing business with country estates and sports clubs, supplying both man-powered and horse-drawn rollers. These firms saw a market for a small motor-powered roller and adapted their established designs of hand or horse rollers to enable them to be driven by a petrol engine. The Barford & Perkins roller with its 8 horsepower Simms engine, a friction clutch and a gearbox, tandem arrangement of rolls and roller chain drive, was the forerunner of many motor rollers produced by this firm. Because it was the first of the line, the roller was christened *Pioneer*, a name which became the Barford & Perkins trademark along with the crossed-picks emblem. The first roller weighed 3 tons and was used successfully for about 23 years. The firm expanded following the success of their small motor rollers and produced ever larger machines, including tandem rollers in stages up to 14 tons. These had rolls which could be filled with water to give a weight difference of up to 2 tons and they were effectively dual-weight machines. A machine of this size became an obvious competitor for the well established steam roller and was favoured by many users.

Barford & Perkins also tried a means of

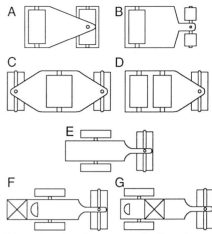

Diagrams of various types of roller: A, tandem; B, semi-tandem; C, early tri-tandem; D, later tri-tandem; E, conventional three-wheel; F, engine behind driver's seat; G, engine in front of driver's seat.

preventing the formation of an undulating road surface by the construction of a tri-tandem roller to the patented design of Colonel R. E. B. Crompton. The prototype, built in 1912, consisted of a three-roll machine fitted with an Astor engine. The two outermost rolls, which steered, were not driven and were slightly smaller in diameter than the centre driving roll and the whole machine weighed around $11^{1}/_{2}$ tons. On trial, the roller produced a road surface with fewer waves than the conventional machines of the time and some were sold on the strength of this, but it was not a great success. This tri-tandem design was later rediscovered on more than one occasion and three-axle steam rollers were also produced (from a conventional Robey tandem roller) but the design was never popular in the rolling trade.

Barford & Perkins continued to develop the small motor roller and just before the First World War produced a conventional three-wheel roller weighing between $1^{1}/_{2}$ and 2 tons in various rolling widths. This was designated the A series and became one of their most popular designs, having a production life, with improvements, of about 35 years.

Robey steam roller, number 45655 of 1930, number 3 in the Wirksworth Quarry Limited fleet, was modified especially for tarmac work by the addition of an extra roll to a tandem roller, making it an unusual tri-tandem. Photographed at Boothstown, Manchester, during the construction works associated with the East Lancs Road (A580) in 1952, it now survives in Devon.

Competition from the Peterborough firm in the small-roller business led Aveling & Porter to produce their own motor roller in 1913, having tried various small steam tandem rollers some time earlier. The use of the latter to the road-rolling contractor was somewhat questionable, although one has survived into the preservation era. Aveling developed their own petrol engine, which was used in their lorries — a design which did not prove very popular — and also in their new range of motor rollers. Unfortunately, as far as is known, no Aveling & Porter motor roller from this period has survived.

Which American firm was the first to produce a motor roller has not so far been established but motor rollers were certainly available by 1907 when one bystander, witnessing one for the first time, was heard to remark: 'Just look at that steam roller running by means of a gasoline motor.' His long acquaintance with rollers powered by steam had obviously served to fix the name in his mind — a notion still with us today. One of the first machines produced in the United States was a light tandem roller whose design owed much to contemporary internal combustion-engined tractor practice.

In an attempt to cash in on the market for light motor rollers T. Green & Son produced a machine very similar to Barford & Perkins's popular A series 2 to 3 ton model. This is either a type MR or LPR of around 1930, of which few, if any, are known to survive.

9

Several Wallis & Steevens steam rollers — this is an Advance type — were exported to India. The members of the roadmaking gang are seen with their picks whilst the roller's tank is replenished with water from an urn. An ox cart enhances this colonial scene outside the Jaipur Hotel.

Two Aveling & Porter steam rollers pause whilst rolling the forecourt of Buckingham Palace, London, at an unknown date. On the left is a 1905 example owned by J. Mowlem & Company, whilst the other is a 6 ton 1896 roller owned by G. Wimpey & Company Limited.

This Aveling & Porter 'coffee pot' steam roller had a vertical boiler and the front roll was driven by a horizontal compound engine mounted on the frame. The driver sat at the rear looking forward past the chimney. Note the Aveling horse trademark on the water tank on the front. This roller is believed to be number 10245 of 1922, an 8 ton tandem.

STEAM-ROLLER MANUFACTURERS

Early in the twentieth century, many traditional traction-engine firms decided there was a market to be found in the steam-roller trade and several of these firms started to manufacture rollers alongside their conventional traction engines, producing machines to what had become the traditional steam-roller design. Competition increased and the demand for rollers became greater during the period of the First World War in order to repair damaged roads and improve communications. Marshall, Burrell and Clayton & Shuttleworth were amongst the manufacturers who started steam-roller production around 1900.

In the years following the First World War other firms joined the booming market but these, such as Armstrong Whitworth, made only a few machines compared with the giants of the steam-roller trade, Aveling & Porter and Fowler. Of the six thousand or so steam rollers produced for the home market, Aveling built about two-thirds and Fowler a tenth.

The slump of the mid 1920s reduced the market and several firms closed down. Others combined forces in an attempt to remain in business. Aveling & Porter joined such an association, known as Agricultural & General Engineers, with Burrell and Garrett in the early 1920s but this was not a happy combination and eventually, after the latter two firms had closed in the early 1930s, Aveling & Porter merged with another AGE partner, their long-time motor-roller rival Barford & Perkins, to form Aveling-Barford in 1934. This was done with financial support from Ruston & Hornsby. The two partners moved their factories from Rochester and Peterborough respectively and the newly combined firm started afresh at Grantham, Lincolnshire, on Ruston & Hornsby land adjacent to the main London & North Eastern Railway line to Scotland. They are still active there today, after further changes in fortune.

As traditional roadmaking techniques changed and tar and bitumen products were used in greater quantities, it was necessary to lay these quickly and without the distortion caused by the slow steam roller stopping and changing direction on top of a newly laid surface. A quick reverse mechanism was developed by Aveling & Porter with their Shay-type tandem roller in 1912; it had the engine mounted vertically on the side. However, an acceptable solution to this problem was not achieved in mass-production form until the early 1920s with the introduction of the Advance design of steam roller by Wallis and Steevens.

After the First World War Aveling & Porter in particular redesigned their standard steam roller and offered a mass-production range of both single and compound machines varying in weight from 6 tons to 20 tons. Customers were able to specify what type of scarifier they required to be fitted to their new roller. Designs available included those by Price, Morrison and Allen.

In order to produce steam rollers more economically, the traditional slide valve, the mechanism by which the steam was admitted to the cylinder, was replaced by a piston valve with piston rings. This was easier to produce and assemble and was said to be more economical in service. Rollers to this design were built in their hundreds in the early 1920s, many being bought by the Eddison Steam Rolling Company, a big rolling contractor. Several of these finished their days in parks and playgrounds for children to play on, having been donated by their last owner, Eddison Plant Limited of Grantham.

A slightly different driving technique was required with piston-valve rollers. It was important to realise that under certain circumstances, because water is incompressible, condensation trapped in the cylinder had to be released before moving the roller. Failure to do this could blow the cylinder cover off or bend the piston rod or valve rod, rendering the roller unserviceable. Many of the old drivers could not come to terms with this new design and so,

A publicity photograph from the Fowler collection depicting a mid 1930s 6-8 ton 'Precision' diesel roller undertaking similar duties to the Leeds Corporation 1903 A4 type 15 ton steam roller number 9703. The latter worked on the city's roads until 1939, when it passed to the firm of W. & J. Glossop of Halifax, who ran it for a few years. It was scrapped by 1949. It is not known how long the demonstrator diesel roller survived.

An early (1923/4) Wallis & Steevens Advance steam roller pictured outside the works at Basingstoke, Hampshire. Note the double high-pressure arrangement of cylinders with inside actuating piston valves, worm and wheel steering and belly tanks with balance pipe. A lifting injector is fitted above the tank — more usually steam rollers have a conventional injector at the base of the tank.

A well engineered motor roller, the 'Precision' type made by Fowler of Leeds in the mid 1930s (maker's number 21323). Despite the machine's fine lines, the firm was late into the motor-roller market and this second design never became popular. Very few motor rollers survive from this well known builder of steam road vehicles.

although it was economical, it did not receive universal acclaim.

Aveling & Porter undertook further redesigning in the late 1920s when the machines were made with larger grates and more tubes, making the rollers easier to steam. They were also fitted with several other improved features including a shorter smokebox for ease of cleaning. Another fundamental design change was to revert to slide valves because these were both efficient and popular. The first of this new design was produced in late 1929. Even today, a driver either likes or dislikes piston valves, usually depending on which kind of steam roller he has driven before.

Both Aveling and Marshall produced tandem rollers fitted with conventional locomotive-type boilers and also the vertical-boilered version. This latter type of boiler gave rise to the nickname of the 'coffee-pot roller'. Some of these were also fitted with a steam-powered steering engine, which was not a suitable mechanism for a novice to operate, such was its complexity of response.

Marshall went on to build the Universal, a roller with similar parameters to the Wallis Advance, but this design does not appear to have been as good as the successful Advance type (and certainly fewer have survived). The Advance used two cylinders of the same size, steam at high pressure acting on both, and it had no flywheel. This arrangement enabled a quick reverse to be achieved. It also had equal pressure on front and rear rolls, direct steering and a clear view from the driver's position in all directions. It was also fitted with a self-cambering back axle and, to order, a double-headed scarifier which could be used at either side. It was perhaps one of the most significant designs of rollers ever made. The diesel version was very close to the steam design and continued in production until 1967. Another popular roller for similar use, although not made in the same quantities, was the Robey tandem with its

There are only a few road steam enthusiasts in the former East Germany. One of them, Gunter Sonntag, kept this sixty-year-old steam roller at Radenburg, north of Dresden, in 1990. The machine is the only known example remaining made by the small builder Lamprecht at Janer i Schles. It is works number 653.

pistol-shaped boiler and stayless firebox.

After the inter-war slump the firms producing large rollers in Britain had dwindled to seven. Fowler's late motor-roller challenge was to no avail and they ceased roller production in 1938 whilst their Leeds contemporary, Thomas Green, had built their last steam roller in 1931 and Wallis & Steevens produced their last in 1940. Marshall's final steam roller was built in 1944 although production continued in India after that date. Aveling-Barford continued selling their new Ruston & Hornsby design until 1948 for the home market and up to 1950 for overseas. This latter design, the Class T steam roller, was subcontracted for construction to a division of Vickers-Armstrong Limited at Newcastle upon Tyne. An era of production lasting some 85 years thus ended in Great Britain but steam rollers continued to be made on the continent for another few years, the French firm of Albaret producing one as late as 1953.

Northampton Corporation steam roller number 1 in their St James Depot in 1951. Locally made by William Allchin Limited in 1900, this is one of only two rollers by that firm known to have survived. Both remain in the Northampton area.

Ipswich Docks Commission owned Armstrong-Whitworth steam roller number 10R22 and used it extensively around the dock complex. Pictured on New Cut West, Ipswich, on 5th March 1936, having been new in 1923, she was in use for some forty years and has survived into the preservation era. She still remains in the Suffolk area.

Looking very much like a contemporary steam roller, this mid 1920s Aveling & Porter crude oil-engined machine was part of the municipal fleet in Colombo, Sri Lanka, where it kept company with several other rollers of a similar vintage.

The manufacturer of this Fordson motor roller conversion is not known but several details of the kit remain. When completed, the unladen weight of the machine was 4 tons 8 cwt (4470 kg), which could be increased by 7 cwt (335 kg) by water ballast in the rolls. The overall length was 123 inches (312 cm) and the width 71 inches (213 cm). The price for this potentially useful machine was £299 when conventional rollers were not readily available during the Second World War. Water is being sprayed from a hose on to the rolls to keep them clean, there being no roll sprays fitted to this utility machine.

A 12 ton (heavy) motor roller of the mid 1930s from Marshall. This is an RD type, which continued in production until after the Second World War. This heavily touched-up 'official' photograph shows it complete with steam-roller style paraffin headlamps.

MOTOR ROLLERS

From the start of the development of motor rollers there were two distinct lines of thought as to what form they might take. On the one hand there was the type with the single-cylinder slow-running engine, as started by Coutant-Dujour and J. G. Allen, later echoed by such classics as the Aveling DX; and on the other hand there were those rollers with the multi-cylinder high-speed engine (by the standards of the time), at first fuelled by petrol or paraffin and later by diesel. This second type was made originally by Barford & Perkins, then by Green and also by Wallis & Steevens. These eventually displaced the single-cylinder rollers and subsequent developments led to the rollers of today. Marshall hedged their bets and made both types and, ever versatile, they were also respected makers of steam rollers for longer than most.

Motor-roller design never became stereotyped in the same way as did that of the steam roller. For example, the final drive could be either gears or chain, whilst the engine could be either ahead of the driver or behind. A device needed on a motor roller which was not required on a steam roller was a foot brake, since the engine could not be reversed for braking as could that of a steam engine. The transmission had to provide for gear changes, for forward and reverse operation and for taking up the drive smoothly in order to set the roller in motion.

There were many variations to accommodate these requirements. Early motor rollers had a single clutch and reversing was effected by declutching, stopping the roller on the foot brake, selecting reverse gear and then letting in the clutch as the foot brake was released. This action caused the roller to pause slightly whilst reversing because the process took a little time, and on tarmac or asphalt surfaces this pause, or 'dwell', allowed the roller to sink slightly into the surface, thus leaving a small wave-like depression in the finished road surface. This arrangement improved in the 1920s when quick reverse transmissions came into general use. These had two clutches, one for forward, the other for reverse. Both were controlled by the same lever so that by its use one clutch was disengaged and the other engaged almost simultaneously and the roller was reversed without dwell time. At least, this was the theory but in practice the driver was required to co-ordinate his use of the clutch lever and foot brake to prevent snatching and a slack driving-chain or sticking clutch taxed his driving skills even further. Nevertheless, this arrangement gave a great improvement in the road surface if used correctly.

The first application of a diesel engine to a road roller was in 1927, when a high-speed diesel engine was fitted to a roller by Barford & Perkins. This date indicates that roller manufacturers were at the forefront of contemporary development as it pre-cedes equivalent innovations in other forms of transport: the first British diesel lorry to go into production was the Kerr Stuart of 1929, which used a six-cylinder Helios en-gine, but this was found to be unsatisfac-tory and was subsequently replaced by a McLaren-Benz engine. Unfortunately, Kerr Stuart went into liquidation in 1930 and the business, designs and patents were acquired by the Hunslet Engine Company Limited of Leeds, who did not pursue the potential road-vehicle market. The first railway locomotive fitted with a diesel en-gine for a British main-line company was an 18 inch (457 mm) gauge Leeds-built Hudswell Clarke which was supplied in 1930 for the London Midland & Scottish Railway's Crewe Works tramway. This also had a McLaren-Benz engine.

There was much scope for designers in the years between the wars and after. It was not unusual for staff to move from one firm to another in order to gain experience and to introduce new designs. Many minor roller makers eagerly competed with the larger firms to supply the smaller rollers needed for sports fields and country estates.

Tractor manufacturers made convertible models whilst other firms in agricultural engineering or car manufacture turned to light motor rollers to diversify into new markets. Three examples of these were Pattison, Brecknell and Singer Cars (Motor Units).

The Second World War enforced a break in development. Most makers introduced austerity rollers, designed to be produced quickly and cheaply. Some of these were based on well tried and tested agricultural designs such as the Fordson tractor and many Green and Aveling-Barford rollers of this type were supplied to the War Min-istry. Marshalls introduced their Utility design roller but some pre-war designs were perpetuated right through the war and afterwards and rollers were built in limited numbers when materials were made avail-able. Because of post-war shortages, roll-ers continued to be made like this for sev-eral years and it was not until the very late 1940s or early in the 1950s that updated designs or even new innovative designs began to emerge.

Since then, designs have provided more comforts for the driver in the form of en-closed cabs, heating and hydraulic steer-ing, as well as scarifiers. Maintenance has also been made easier with the introduction of various types of hydraulic transmissions. Rubber-tyred rollers, for chippings, also became popular. Traditional items such as cone clutches, chain drives, hand starting and single-cylinder engines were thus dis-carded although many rollers with these features still remain in preservation.

There has been in more recent years a swing away from the traditional three-wheel deadweight roller in favour of the lighter tandem vibrating roller, with con-sequent economies, but it is still questioned in some circles as to whether a vibrating roller achieves as good a compaction of the roadway as a deadweight machine.

West Riding County Council steam roller number 5, pictured on Rigg Lane, Garforth, Leeds, in the mid 1920s during a road-widening job. WR 6808 was Ruston & Hornsby roller number 52785, built in Lincoln in 1920.

THE ROADMAKERS

Road rollers were bought by local councils in charge of highway maintenance and also by road-rolling contractors. Until the 1880s local highway boards were the responsible authorities but, with local government reorganisation, urban district, city and county councils became responsible for the upkeep of roads in their areas. Contractors worked either for the landowners in the vicinity or for the council if its own roller was under repair or it did not have one of its own. In the early years of the twentieth century and again after the First World War rollers were in such demand that large fleets were built up by such firms as Eddison, Lancashire Steam Rolling Company, John Allen of Oxford, Buncombe of Highbridge, Somerset, and Dingle from Cornwall; vast areas were covered by men in their employment.

The roller, its living van and water cart were a familiar road train in the countryside as they went from job to job; the driver, his wife and often his family too lived in the van for long periods. Some of the large contractors ran as many as two hundred rollers at their peak but there was always

work for the small contractor with just a few rollers. This type of contractor was to be found nationwide, serving those who required only relatively small areas resurfacing and sometimes, in more recent times, working for a larger contractor when the necessity arose. There was always also a place for the owner-driver and many flourished for a long time, one continuing in Yorkshire until 1984.

To prepare a firm base for a road, large stones are put down and rolled, their irregular shapes being pushed together and locked in position. Smaller stones are put on top and the process repeated. The raw materials are usually quarried and then reduced in size by a stone crusher. In the early days roadside stonebreaking was undertaken by old men, women and children who sat at the side of the road to break up the stones. Later the powered crusher was used, initially driven by a steam portable engine and then by a traction engine, which could also haul it from place to place. The steam roller made the job of compacting the stones very much easier.

Clayton & Shuttleworth steam roller number 48792 owned by W. W. Buncombe of Highbridge, Somerset, in a West Suffolk lane, parked up, awaiting its next turn of duty. The sign, flag and living van depict a tranquil scene which could have been photographed at almost any time within a forty-year period.

Marshall steam roller number 84620 at work near Hull in 1951. Haltemprice Urban District Council purchased the roller new in 1929 and it remained with them until disposed of by tender in the early 1960s.

One of W. W. Buncombe's fleet of steam rollers, number 150, far from the firm's premises at Highbridge, Somerset. It was pictured in 1950 at Hadleigh, Suffolk, with a typical contractor's living van in tow. Aveling & Porter number 14147 is in preservation and is rallied in southern England.

In the late 1880s the road's top surface was produced by water binding. The steam roller first compacted the broken stone before dust was added to form a top surface, which was watered and rolled. By working the top surface to a slurry and then leaving it to dry, a fine hard finish was achieved. To rework a road of this nature, a scarifier was used, dragging along picks or tines which could be wound down into the road surface to dig it up. Scarifiers could be engine-mounted but sometimes a trailed

A promotional postcard from W. Shepherd & Sons, tarmacadam contractors, Milkstone, Rochdale, depicts an unusual Marshall-Millar design of vertical-boilered tandem steam roller. The drive, by bevel gears (two-speed), to the rear roll from the vertical engine is clearly seen. The wooden wheelbarrow and rake are typical of the contractor's tools used for resurfacing work.

'Cinderella' poses for a photograph in the early years of the twentieth century. Owned by Hampshire Brothers of Ravensthorpe, West Yorkshire, this early single-cylinder Aveling steam roller is at work in a railway goods yard somewhere in the West Riding of Yorkshire. During the First World War, this roller was commandeered for military work and is believed to have been sunk and lost during her transfer abroad.

David Wood of Yeadon, Leeds, used this 1920 Fowler steam roller extensively in North Yorkshire on tar-spraying duties. A pump mounted on the left-hand belly tank was driven by a chain from the flywheel boss and delivered hot tar to the spray bar on the rear. To achieve an even coating on the road surface, a rotary brush, also chain-driven, was used. The tar tank is being replenished in the course of a resurfacing contract in north Leeds. The roller survives in North Yorkshire.

Hampshire Brothers were a small Yorkshire contracting firm dating back to the mid nineteenth century. Aveling steam roller number 4800 of 1900 was on hire to a local council sometime before requiring to be registered (in 1921). Driver Willie Lockwood stands proudly on the left, with one of the original Hampshire brothers next to him. This roller, named 'Busybody', was fitted with a three-tine reversible scarifier.

independent scarifier was towed behind the roller. There were always difficulties in reversing such a scarifier at the end of the pull. When the road had been dug up, it was levelled by hand and re-rolled. Independent scarifiers were used in the West Country until the 1960s as they could reach the middle of narrow lanes, inaccessible to other types at the time.

As private cars proliferated and heavier lorries were introduced in the years before the First World War, the speeds of road

traffic increased and it became necessary to lay the dust which was a feature of water-bound roads. Asphalt and tar-based surfacing materials began to be used in road construction and the tar, used as a binder for the top layers of fine stone or gravel, had to be heated in a tar boiler. Sometimes these boilers were heated by steam from the hauling engine; others had their own coal fire.

Tar-coated stone was usually produced in a mixer and laid by hand before being rolled. After the Second World War bitumen-coated

A trailed independent scarifier of the Thackray type, manufactured by Barford & Perkins of Peterborough. It was towed behind the roller, being steered by the tiller at the rear to one side of the road or the other. This is a two-tine machine which is also fitted with a hand brake.

stone (bitmac) became more popular and the paving machine which laid a strip at a time, automatically, was introduced.

One method of top dressing used in the earlier years of the twentieth century was tarring and chipping. In many places this is still seen today as a cheap means of restoring a worn road surface. Rubber-tyred motor rollers became popular for this purpose and they would follow the gritting lorry to push the chippings into the tarred road surface. Motorists loathe this method since loose chippings which are not swept up quickly after the application can be thrown up by other speeding vehicles and many windscreens have been broken as a result.

In the first application of this method, a traction engine drew a tar tank which sprayed the hot tar on to the road surface. This was then followed by a team of men with shovels, throwing the chippings with a flicking motion to get an even spread before the steam roller came along to embed the chippings into the hot tar and finish the job.

Later, a combined steam roller and tar sprayer which towed a gritting machine was developed by the contractor David Wood of Yeadon, Leeds, and in conjunction with Fowler several of these outfits were supplied to other contractors in Britain and abroad. At the end of the days of steam, Sentinel steam waggons were used extensively as tar sprayers, being followed by a lorry carrying the chippings, which fell through a hopper and automatically were spread evenly on to the road. Steam rollers gave way to motor rollers — it was hard work chasing the gritter — and they were easier to handle and faster, too. The Sentinel waggon, especially popular with the firm of W. & J. Glossop Limited of Halifax, West Yorkshire, was also eventually ousted by the motor lorry.

Today, basic roadmaking and occasionally tarring and chipping are demonstrated using traditional methods and equipment at steam events around Britain by members of the Road Roller Association. In order that such skills are not lost, training courses are also run by the Association in the art of roadmaking and the use of a road roller as a roadmaking tool.

This period roadmaking scene, of tarring and chipping with the Fowler steam roller waiting in the background to complete the job, was a 1988 re-creation at the Black Country Museum, Dudley, West Midlands, as part of a roadmaking demonstration by the members of the Road Roller Association in appropriate costume.

A pause in the patching demonstration being undertaken by 1911 Barford & Perkins model D3 motor roller at Bramham Park Traction Engine Rally enables Lyndon Shearman to discuss the next move with driver Peter Lorimer, both then Road Roller Association members.

A working demonstration of tar spraying and gritting at Lightwater Valley near Ripon, North Yorkshire, using a 1920 Fowler steam roller, a Coleman 'Flapper' tar boiler and a 1911 Barford & Perkins model D3 motor roller. The living van is one of the few surviving artefacts of the once large firm of David Wood & Company, Yeadon, Leeds, to whom the Fowler roller also belonged at one time.

Above left: *A quaint 'one-off' 1 ton steam roller built in 1933 by A. W. Trotter of Coleford, Gloucestershire. It is believed the engine is from either a boat or a steam bus. The rolls were made from flat belt pulleys. It is now in the care of Gloucester City Museums.*

Above right: *The stern figure seated on this electrically powered roller is believed to be the principal of Thomas Green & Son, Leeds; the location is perhaps the garden of his north Leeds house and the date is c. 1905. The current came from an overhead supply and the primitive motor drove through a worm and wheel arrangement via a chain to the rear rolls. Steering was by tiller.*

Below left: *Pedal power in the garden of the White House, Barsham, Suffolk, about 1912-13. The man in the driving seat is believed to be the inventor, Arthur Samuel Francis Robinson. This was the forerunner of the Motor Units motor roller. Note the sunshade to protect the driver!*

Below right: *A publicity photograph taken in 1935 at Canterbury Street Works, Coventry, the home of Singer Cars, with a new Motor Units motor roller showing its capability in the compaction of gravel or cinders in the car park. The new improved version of the following year cost £10 more and had a smaller-diameter three-section front roll and other minor modifications.*

Edward Pratt's 1889 human-powered roller, exhibited at the Royal Agricultural Society's Exhibition, Windsor, Berkshire. By turning the crank handle, through a series of gears, the men were able to propel the machine slowly along. The weight of the roller could be varied up to 5 tons by means of removable weights.

UNCONVENTIONAL ROLLERS

Rollers powered by oil or steam engines are regarded today as commonplace but, notwithstanding that some steam rollers were of a most unusual design, there have been other means of propulsion devised for rollers.

In 1889 Edward Pratt of the Albert Iron Works, Uxbridge, Middlesex, exhibited two rollers at the Royal Agricultural Society's Exhibition at Windsor. The first of these machines was hand-powered, worked by one or more men who travelled on it, turning a wheel or crank handle. The second was a horse-powered machine in which the horse walked along a treadmill. It was claimed that both of these relatively light types of roller had one advantage over conventional hauled rollers of the time, in that footmarks were not left behind by the men or horses pulling them. This was of particular value for lawns and gravel paths, although the rate of progress was, of necessity, somewhat slow. They did not become popular.

In about 1905 the Leeds firm of Thomas Green & Son produced an electric-powered roller using an early open-coil type of motor; the current collection may have been through a trolley pole arrangement or a suspended trailing cable. Although the oper-ating voltage is not known, the dangers of such a machine on damp grass or in the rain are obvious.

Arthur Samuel Francis Robinson, a gentleman inventor from Barsham, Beccles, Suffolk, patented a pedal-powered, wooden-framed garden roller in 1909 and made a successful working machine which he used to roll the lawns of his residence, The White House, in the years before the First World War. The original patent specification called for a bicycle frame as the basis of the roller although this was later improved upon. The patented means of driving the rear rolls was by chains from dog clutches on a layshaft, arranged with cam-operating arms from the steering pillar in order to give a differential effect when corners were turned. This system was carried right through his various patents until a motorised version was proposed in 1926. This finally went into production as the 10 cwt (508 kg) Motor Units roller in the mid 1930s.

Wallis & Steevens produced a small sloping-boilered 3 ton steam roller in the mid 1920s. This was named the Simplicity. Unfortunately it made no impact on the market for small rollers since by that time this was monopolised by the makers of motor

The operator is dwarfed by this huge Marshall-built special-purpose four-wheel steam roller made for earth compaction on reservoir embankments for County Durham Waterworks. The power was derived from a vertical Sentinel boiler, more usually to be found on a steam waggon or shunting locomotive, and a horizontal engine.

This non-powered rubber-tyred roller was developed during the Second World War. It was relatively lightweight (for easier transport) but could be heavily ballasted with water or other locally obtained materials to increase its weight. It was towed by a tractor or military vehicle. Good compaction was achieved as the wheels were mounted eccentrically and they also pivoted from side to side, the device being hence known as a 'wobbly wheel roller'. It came in nine-, eleven- and thirteen-wheel versions and was used with great success in producing forward airstrips and keeping them in good order in France after D Day and later in the Western Desert, having been made in great numbers in the USA, and also in England by Pullen Engineering, London. They were used commercially throughout the world after the war.

rollers. Six of this unusual type of steam roller remain in preservation in Britain.

A small number of huge four-wheeled rollers were built by Marshall specially for compacting earth on reservoir construction contracts. The rolls on these machines were around 12 feet (3.7 metres) in diameter and the power was derived from a vertical Sentinel steam-waggon type boiler and engine mounted in the centre of a large base frame. John Allen & Sons produced a caterpillar-tracked style roller in 1929, again using a Sentinel boiler, the machine being called the Waveless roller. It had a large flat area in contact with the ground — a departure from the usual cylindrical roll used since the inception of the road roller. It did not find favour when built but was nearly thirty years ahead of its time, for conventional caterpillar tractors were used for consolidation purposes on motorway construction in the 1960s.

This inclined-boiler design 'Simplicity' steam roller was the prototype and was made by Wallis & Steevens in 1926. It is pictured in the approaches to Basingstoke railway yard, adjacent to the Wallis works, before delivery to its first owner, a contractor in London. Number 7832 is preserved in Somerset.

SOME ROAD-ROLLER MANUFACTURERS

Acme Road Machinery Company Incorporated, Frankfort, New York, USA.

A. B. Akerman, Eslöv, Sweden.

S. A. des Ans Ets Albaret, Ratigny and Liancourt, France.

William Allchin & Company, Northampton.

John Allen & Sons Limited, Oxford.

J. G. Allen & Company, Belfast and Dublin, Ireland.

U. Ammann Maschinenfabrik AG, Langenthal, Switzerland.

Aktiebolage Abjorn Anderson, Svedala, Sweden.

Ansaldo e Cia, Genoa, Italy.

Armstrong-Holland, Sydney, Australia.

Sir W. G. Armstrong-Whitworth & Company Limited, Manchester.

Austin Manufacturing Company, Chicago, Illinois, USA.

Austral-Otis, Melbourne, Australia.

Auto-Mower Engineering Company Limited, Bath, Avon.

Aveling-Barford Limited, Grantham, Lincolnshire.

Aveling & Porter Limited, Rochester, Kent.

The Avery Company, Peoria, Illinois, USA.

Babcock & Wilcox Limited, Lincoln.

Banting, Toledo, Ohio, USA.

Barber Asphalt Company, Philadelphia, Pennsylvania, USA.

Barford & Perkins Limited, Peterborough, Cambridgeshire.

Bell, Seaforth, Ontario, Canada.

Blackburn, London.

Bray, Folkestone, Kent.

H. Brecknell & Sons Limited, Keynsham, Bristol.

Soc Ernesto Breda, Milan, Italy.

Buffalo Springfield Roller Company, Springfield, Ohio, USA.

Charles Burrell & Sons Limited, Thetford, Norfolk.

Casa Metager, Spain.

J. I. Case Threshing Machine Company Incorporated, Racine, Wisconsin, USA.

Cegielski, Poznan, Poland.

Ceskomoravska-Kolbern-Danek (Praga), Prague, Czechoslovakia.

Alexander Chaplin & Company, Glasgow, Scotland.

Chataignier et Compagnie, St Etienne, France.

Clayton & Shuttleworth Limited, Lincoln.

Motorenfabrik Deutz, Cologne, Germany.

Dewind-Inglis, Toronto, Canada.

Eddington & Steevenson, Chelmsford, Essex.
Maschinenfabrik Esslingen, Esslingen, Germany.
Fisken Brothers, Leeds, West Yorkshire.
Florisdorf, Vienna, Austria.
John Fowler & Company Limited, Leeds, West Yorkshire.
Société Française, Vierzon, France.
Galion Iron Works & Manufacturing Company, Galion, Ohio, USA.
Richard Garrett & Sons Limited, Leiston, Suffolk.
Good Roads Machinery Company Incorporated, Philadelphia, Pennsylvania, USA.
Thomas Green & Son Limited, Leeds, West Yorkshire.
Gebruder Hamm, Tirschenreuth, Bavaria, Germany.
Heilbronn, Heilbronn, Germany.
A. Henninger, Darmstadt, Germany.
Henschel und Sohn GmbH, Kassel, Germany.
Huber Manufacturing Company, Marion, Ohio, USA.
Installaciones Industriales, Bilbao, Spain.
Iroquois Iron Company, Buffalo, New York, USA.
Jelbart Engineers, Ballarat, Victoria, Australia.
Meisenor Jensen, Malmo, Sweden.
Arn Jung, Jungenthal bei Kirchen am Sieg, Germany.
Karl Kaelble GmbH, Backnang, Germany.
Kant Bauverwaltung, Germany.
Kastrup, Denmark.
J. Kemna, Breslau, Germany (now Wroclaw, Poland).
G. Kuhn, Germany.
Ets Laffly, Billancourt, Paris, France.
Lamprecht, Janer i Schles, Germany.
Heinrich Lanz AG, Mannheim, Germany.
A. H. Macdonald & Company Proprietary Limited, Melbourne, Australia.
J. A. Maffei AG (later Krauss-Maffei), Munich and Leipzig, Germany.
Mann's Patent Steam Cart & Wagon Company Limited, Leeds, West Yorkshire.
Maquinista Fabrica Terrestre y Maritima, Barcelona, Spain.
Marshall, Sons & Company Limited, Gainsborough, Lincolnshire.

Massey Sawyer, Hamilton, Ontario, Canada.
J. & H. McLaren Limited, Leeds, West Yorkshire.
Monarch Roller Company, Groton, New York, USA.
Motor Units Limited, Coventry, West Midlands.
Munktells Mekanista Werkstad, Eskilstuna, Sweden.
H. R. Nash & Company Limited, Dorking, Surrey.
Theodor Ohl, Diez and Limburg an der Lahn, Germany.
H. Pattison & Company Limited, Stanmore, Middlesex.
Port Huron Engine & Thresher Company, Port Huron, Michigan, USA.
Pullen Engineering Company Limited, London.
Puricelli, Milan, Italy.
Richier, Charleville, France.
Robey & Company Limited, Lincoln.
Ruston & Hornsby Limited, Lincoln.
Ruston Proctor & Company Limited, Lincoln.
B. Ruthemeyer, Soest, Germany.
L. Schwartzkopff, Berlin, Germany.
Schweitzerische Locomotive und Maschinenfabrik, Winterthur, Switzerland.
Stothert & Pitt Limited, Bath, Avon.
William Tasker & Sons Limited, Andover, Hampshire.
H. Thiadens, Stadskanaal, Holland.
Thompson's Engineering & Pipe Company, Castlemaine, Victoria, Australia.
Trusty Tractors (London) Limited, Barnet, Hertfordshire.
Via (Aktiebolag June Verken), Bankeryd, Sweden.
Volund, Denmark.
Wallis & Steevens Limited, Basingstoke, Hampshire.
Waterous Engine Works, Brantford, Ontario, Canada.
Wehr Company, Milwaukee, Wisconsin, USA.
Winschoter Industrie Mij, Winschoten, Holland.
Maschinenfabrik Hubert Zettelmeyer, Konz bei Trier, Germany.

FURTHER READING

Aveling-Barford Limited. *A Hundred Years of Road Rollers.* Oakwood Press, 1965.
Bonnet, H. *Traction Engines.* Shire, 1985, updated 1990.
Crawley, J. *Traction Engines in Focus.* John Crawley Limited, 1982.
Crawley, J. *Steam Rollers in Focus.* John Crawley Limited, 1986.
Georgano, G. N. *The World's Commercial Vehicles 1830-1964.* Temple Press, 1965.
Gladwin, D. *Steam on the Road.* Batsford, 1988.
Sherwen, T. *The Bomford Story.* Bomford (private), 1978.
True, J. B. *Traction Engine Register.* Southern Counties Historic Vehicle Preservation Trust, 1987; updated 1992.
Wise, D. B. *Steam on the Road.* Hamlyn, 1973.
Whitehead, R. A. *A Century of Service — An Illustrated History of Eddison Plant Ltd.* Eddison Plant Limited, 1968.
Whitehead, R. A. *A Century of Steam Rolling.* Ian Allan, 1975.
Whitehead, R. A. *Wallis & Steevens — A History.* Road Locomotive Society, 1983.

PLACES TO VISIT

Collections of road rollers may be found at the following museums, where one or more may be displayed. It is advisable to check that relevant items are on show, as well as to find out opening times, before making a special journey, in order to avoid disappointment.

UNITED KINGDOM

Amberley Chalk Pits Museum, Houghton Bridge, Amberley, Arundel, West Sussex BN18 9LT. Telephone: 0798 831370.
Beamish: The North of England Open Air Museum, Beamish, Stanley, County Durham DH9 0RG. Telephone: 0207 231811.
Birmingham Museum of Science and Industry, Newhall Street, Birmingham, West Midlands B3 1RZ. Telephone: 021-236 1022.
Bradford Industrial Museum, Moorside Road, Eccleshill, Bradford, West Yorkshire BD2 3HP. Telephone: 0274 631756.
Bressingham Steam Museum, Bressingham, Diss, Norfolk IP22 2AB. Telephone: 037988 382 or 386.
East Anglia Transport Museum, Chapel Road, Carlton Colville, Lowestoft, Suffolk NR33 9BL. Telephone: 0502 518459.
Glasgow Museum of Transport, Kelvin Hall, 1 Bunhouse Road, Glasgow G3 8PZ. Telephone: 041-357 3929.
Hampshire County Museums Service, Chilcombe House, Chilcombe Lane, Winchester, Hampshire SO23 8RD. Telephone: 0962 66242. Visits by appointment only.
Hollycombe Steam Collection, Hollycombe House, Liphook, Hampshire. Telephone: 0428 723233.
Klondyke Mill Steam Museum, Draycott in the Clay, Staffordshire.
Leeds Industrial Museum, Armley Mills, Canal Road, Armley, Leeds, West Yorkshire LS12 2QF. Telephone: 0532 637861.
Leicester Museum of Technology, Abbey Pumping Station, Corporation Road, Abbey Lane, Leicester. Telephone: 0533 661330.
Liverpool Museum, William Brown Street, Liverpool, Merseyside L3 8EN. Telephone: 051-207 0001.
The Long Shop Museum, Main Street, Leiston, Suffolk. Telephone: 0728 830550 or 832189.
Strumpshaw Hall Steam Museum, Hall Farm, Low Road, Strumpshaw, Norwich, Norfolk NR13 4HS. Telephone: 0603 714535.

Summerlee Heritage Trust, West Canal Street, Coatbridge, Lanarkshire ML5 1QD. Telephone: 0236 31261.
The Thursford Collection, Thursford, Fakenham, Norfolk NR21 0AS. Telephone: 0328 878477.
Ulster Folk and Transport Museum, Witham Street Gallery, Newtownards Road, Belfast, Northern Ireland BT4 1HP. Telephone: 0232 451519.

EUROPE
Auto + Technik Museum, Obere Au 2, 6920 Sinsheim bei Heidelberg, Germany.
Maschinistenschool SOMA, Kerkweg 59, Ede, Gelderland, Holland.

In addition, several individual rollers are located in playgrounds, parks and other similar places with free access — in many cases having been put there through the generosity of their previous owners — for the recreational benefit of the local children. Recent more rigorous safety legislation is resulting in a gradual reduction in these rollers. Some locations where 'parked up' rollers have been reported are: Cluny Square, Southend, Essex; Lifstan Way, Southend, Essex; Wyndham Park, Grantham, Lincolnshire; Victoria Park, Leamington Spa, Warwickshire; Dorchester, Dorset; Cambridge Park, Guernsey; West Drayton, Middlesex; Seacroft, Leeds; Aberfeldy, Tayside; Belle View Park, Wrexham, Clwyd; Goole, Humberside; Leisure Centre, Aviemore, Highland.

THE ROAD ROLLER ASSOCIATION
The Association was formed in 1974 by a few dedicated enthusiasts with the prime objective of encouraging the preservation of rollers powered by either steam or internal combustion engine, living vans, water carts, tar boilers and other equipment used for road construction. Not all members are roller owners and it is not necessary to be one to become a member. The Association welcomes all with an interest in roadmaking in all its various forms. A quarterly magazine called *Rolling* is produced, full of useful and sometimes humorous articles.
Anyone interested in steam or motor rollers should be a member. Further details from: Mrs A. S. Arrowsmith, Secretary, Road Roller Association, 7 Worcester Close, Lichfield, Staffordshire WS13 7SP.

The 'Tractamount' roller, manufactured by Twose of Tiverton, Devon, was a non-powered attachment, capable of converting a conventional tractor into a roller of some 3¹/₂ to 8 tons capacity, depending on model and ballasting. The drive to the roller wheels was by chain from a bolted-on axle extension on each side of the tractor. An additional steering wheel and shaft were used to turn the attachment's front rolls. The ramp arrangement for loading the tractor, piggy-back style, is shown in this tropical scene.